The Hole Truth!
Underground
Animal Life

Gila Monster's Burrow

by Dee Phillips

Consultants:

Stephen Hammack
Herpetarium Keeper, St. Louis Zoo, St. Louis, Missouri

Kimberly Brenneman, PhD
National Institute for Early Education Research, Rutgers University, New Brunswick, New Jersey

BEARPORT
PUBLISHING

New York, New York

Credits

Cover, © Rick & Nora Bowers/Alamy; 2–3, © fivespots/Shutterstock; 4, © Wayne Lynch/All Canada Photos/Superstock; 5, © Minden Pictures/Superstock; 6T, © Jared Hobbs/All Canada Photos/Superstock; 7, © Rick & Nora Bowers/Alamy; 8, © reptiles4all/Shutterstock; 9, © Eric Isselee/Shutterstock, © Darren J. Bradley/Shutterstock, © Richard A. McMillin/Shutterstock, and © gkuna/Shutterstock; 10, © George H. H. Huey/Alamy; 11, © Carlos Sanz/Visual & Written SL/Alamy; 12, © David Hosking/FLPA; 13, © John Cancalosi/Alamy; 14, © ZSSD/Minden Pictures/FLPA; 15, © Daniel Heuclin/Nature Picture Library; 16, © blickwinkel/Alamy; 17, © Visuals Unlimited/Nature Picture Library; 18–19, © Thomas Wiewandt/Wildhorizons.com; 20, © Rick & Nora Bowers/Alamy; 21, © Krzysztof Wiktor/Shutterstock; 22L, © fivespots/Shutterstock; 22R, © ANCH/Shutterstock; 23TL, © Carlos Sanz/Visual & Written SL/Alamy; 23TC, © bjul/Shutterstock; 23TR, © blickwinkel/Alamy; 23BL, © Matt Jeppson/Shutterstock; 23BC, © Jared Hobbs/All Canada Photos/Superstock; 23BR, © Minden Pictures/Superstock.

Publisher: Kenn Goin
Editorial Director: Adam Siegel
Creative Director: Spencer Brinker
Design: Emma Randall
Editor: Jessica Rudolph
Photo Researcher: Ruby Tuesday Books Ltd

Library of Congress Cataloging-in-Publication Data

Phillips, Dee, 1967- author.
  Gila monster's burrow / by Dee Phillips.
      pages cm. -- (The hole truth!: underground animal life)
  Includes bibliographical references and index.
  ISBN-13: 978-1-62724-309-4 (library binding)
  ISBN-10: 1-62724-309-7 (library binding)
1. Gila monster--Behavior--Juvenile literature. 2. Gila monster--Habitations--Juvenile literature.
3. Gila monster--Life cycles--Juvenile literature. I. Title.
  QL666.L247P45 2015
  597.95'952156--dc23
                          2014017380

For more information, write to Bearport Publishing Company, Inc., 45 West 21st Street, Suite 3B, New York, New York 10010. Printed in the United States of America.

Contents

Meet a Gila Monster

It's a summer evening in a **desert**.

From a hole beneath some rocks, a large pink-and-black animal appears.

It's a Gila monster.

The animal has been in its **burrow** all day to protect itself from the hot sun.

As night falls, it heads off into the cool darkness to hunt for food.

burrow

Gila monster

Gila monster

The word *Gila* is pronounced "HEE-lah." A Gila monster is a type of lizard. Long ago, people named these lizards monsters because they wrongly believed the lizards attacked and killed humans.

How would you describe a Gila monster to someone who has never seen one?

5

All About Gila Monsters

A Gila monster has a large head, short legs, and a fat tail.

Its body is covered with **scales**.

On parts of the lizard's body, the scales look like small beads.

Many of a Gila monster's scales are black.

The others are pink, orange, or yellow.

Gila monsters live in deserts, where few plants grow.

Gila monster scales

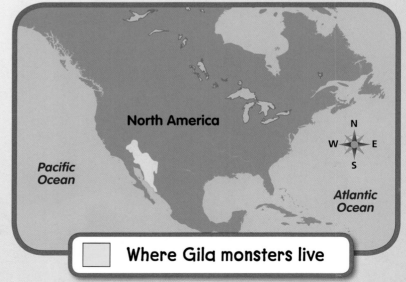

North America

Pacific Ocean

Atlantic Ocean

N
W E
S

Where Gila monsters live

Gila monsters belong to a group of animals called **reptiles**. All reptiles are cold-blooded. This means their body temperatures rise and drop with the temperature of the air around them.

An adult Gila monster is about 21.5 inches (55 cm) long from its nose to the end of its tail. Find this number on a measuring tape to see how long the lizard is in real life.

A Gila Monster's Homes

A Gila monster usually uses two burrows.

It digs one burrow in a cool place to use as a shelter during spring and summer.

It digs a second burrow in a warmer area to use during fall and winter.

To make a burrow, a Gila monster finds a place with lots of rocks.

Then it uses its strong claws to dig a hole under the rocks.

Sometimes a Gila monster uses a burrow dug by another animal. For example, the lizard might find a desert tortoise's burrow. If the tortoise no longer lives in the burrow, the Gila monster moves in!

claw

entrance hole

burrow

9

A Burrow for Keeping Cool

A Gila monster uses its burrows in different ways during the year.

In spring, it sleeps in a burrow at night and spends the day outside.

When summer comes, however, the desert gets very hot.

So the lizard spends the daytime resting underground to keep cool.

At night, the Gila monster leaves its home to go hunting.

a Gila monster looking for food in spring

a Gila monster leaving its burrow after dark in summer

Gila monsters live in some of the hottest places on Earth. During summer, daytime temperatures in the deserts where the lizards live may reach 120°F (49°C).

A Burrow for Keeping Warm

As summer ends, a Gila monster moves to its winter burrow.

During the fall, it hunts by day and sleeps underground at night.

When winter comes, the desert gets very cold.

So the lizard spends the winter months resting underground in its burrow.

It doesn't leave its home again until the weather warms up in spring.

fat tail

During winter, a Gila monster eats nothing! In warmer months, it stores in its tail lots of fat from food. While it is underground all winter, its body lives off this fat.

a Gila monster in its burrow

What kinds of foods do you think Gila monsters eat?

What's on the Menu?

Gila monsters leave their burrows to hunt for mice, rats, frogs, small lizards, and baby birds.

They also eat insects, worms, and birds' eggs.

A Gila monster uses its tongue to smell for food.

As it slowly walks around the desert, it flicks its tongue in the air.

Once it smells a meal, it sneaks up on the animal and attacks!

tongue

When a Gila monster finds a small animal to eat, the lizard grabs it with its powerful jaws. Then the Gila monster swallows the animal whole.

bird egg

Gila Monster Eggs

In spring, male and female Gila monsters come together to **mate**.

About eight weeks after mating, a female Gila monster lays her eggs.

Using her claws, she digs a shallow hole in the ground.

She lays between 2 and 12 eggs in the hole.

Then she covers them with sand.

a pair of Gila monsters

After laying her eggs, a female Gila monster leaves them. She does not take care of her eggs or her babies after they hatch.

a female Gila monster laying eggs

egg

Gila monster eggs have soft, leathery shells. The eggs in this picture are life-size. Use a ruler to measure how big they are.

(The answer is on page 24.)

Mini Monsters

It takes about four months for baby Gila monsters to grow inside their eggs.

When they are ready to hatch, they break out of their eggs.

Then they crawl up through the sand to the surface.

The little Gila monsters look just like their parents—but much smaller!

A baby Gila monster is just over six inches (15 cm) long. It weighs about the same as seven quarters.

baby Gila monster

a baby Gila monster hatching from an egg

If a Gila monster lays her eggs in April and it takes four months for the babies to grow, in what month will the babies hatch?

(The answer is on page 24.)

Growing Up

When they hatch, baby Gila monsters take care of themselves.

They find eggs and insects to eat.

To keep cool in summer and warm in winter, they take shelter in small holes or in cracks between rocks.

As they get bigger and stronger, they start to dig burrows.

At three years old, they are adults—and ready for their grown-up lives in the desert!

a young Gila monster

bird egg

Both adult and baby Gila monsters have **venomous** bites. Their small teeth are covered with venom, or poison. The lizards can use their dangerous bite to protect themselves against coyotes and large birds that try to eat them.

teeth

Science Lab

A Gila Monster's Year

Make a calendar that shows a year in a Gila monster's life.

Divide the calendar into four parts—spring, summer, fall, and winter.

In each section of the calendar, write facts and draw pictures to show the things a lizard might do during that season.

Use the information in this book to help you.

A Gila Monster Calendar

 Spring

A female Gila monster lays eggs.

 Summer

Baby Gila monsters hatch from their eggs.

 Fall

Winter

A Gila monster stays underground.

It lives off the fat that's stored in its tail.

Science Words

burrow (BUR-oh) a hole or tunnel dug by an animal to live in

desert (DEZ-urt) dry land with few plants and little rainfall; some deserts are covered with sand

mate (MAYT) to come together in order to have young

reptiles (REP-tilez) cold-blooded animals, such as lizards and snakes, that have scaly skin

scales (SKALEZ) small pieces of hard skin that cover the body of a reptile, such as a lizard or snake

venomous (VEN-uhm-uhss) able to attack with a poisonous bite or sting

Index

Read More

Clark, Willow. *Gila Monster! (Animal Danger Zone)*. New York: Windmill Books (2011).

Lunis, Natalie. *Komodo Dragon: The World's Biggest Lizard (SuperSized!)*. New York: Bearport (2007).

Townsend, Emily Rose. *Lizards (Desert Animals)*. Mankato, MN: Pebble Books (2004).

Learn More Online

To learn more about Gila monsters, visit **www.bearportpublishing.com/TheHoleTruth!**

About the Author

Dee Phillips lives near the ocean on the southwest coast of England. She develops and writes nonfiction and fiction books for children of all ages.

Answers

Page 17: The eggs are about 2 to 2.5 inches (5 to 6.4 cm) long.
Page 19: The babies will hatch from their eggs in August.